THE STRANGE TRAVELS OF SVINHILDE WILSON

The Strange Travels of Svinhilde Wilson

A collection of poems
by

STEPHANIE V SEARS

Adelaide Books
New York / Lisbon
2020

THE STRANGE TRAVELS OF SVINHILDE WILSON

A collection of poems

by Stephanie V Sears

Published by Adelaide Books, New York / Lisbon
adelaidebooks.org

Editor-in-Chief
Stevan V. Nikolic

For any information, please address Adelaide Books
at info@adelaidebooks.org

or write to:

Adelaide Books
244 Fifth Ave. Suite D27
New York, NY, 10001

ISBN: 978-1-952570-90-2

Printed in the United States of America

Contents

Poems previously published in literary reviews

At Clark's Pool, Summer Noon, Through the Rain, Basilica, Momentary Death, The Sanctuary,Tropic, Lagoon, Above the Plain of Finnmark, A Place in Sweden, Fog of the Sundarbans, Havelock Island, Posada of Creeping Horror, Venetian Winter, Far Into the Night, Bay of Invisible Merits, Mt Gower, Summer Storm, Seaborn, A Favorable Moon, After the Ice Age, Polynesian Morning, Brought Back, Illumination on the Tatai, The Forgotten Temple, Over Bangkok, Bear River, Passing Through Venice, Cross Country, Lithuanian Transposition, Art Full, No Speeding, At Saint David's, The Puzzle, Antiquity, The Archeologist Gone Mad, Onto Itself, Going Back to Versailles Yellow Silk, There's Good in that Devil.

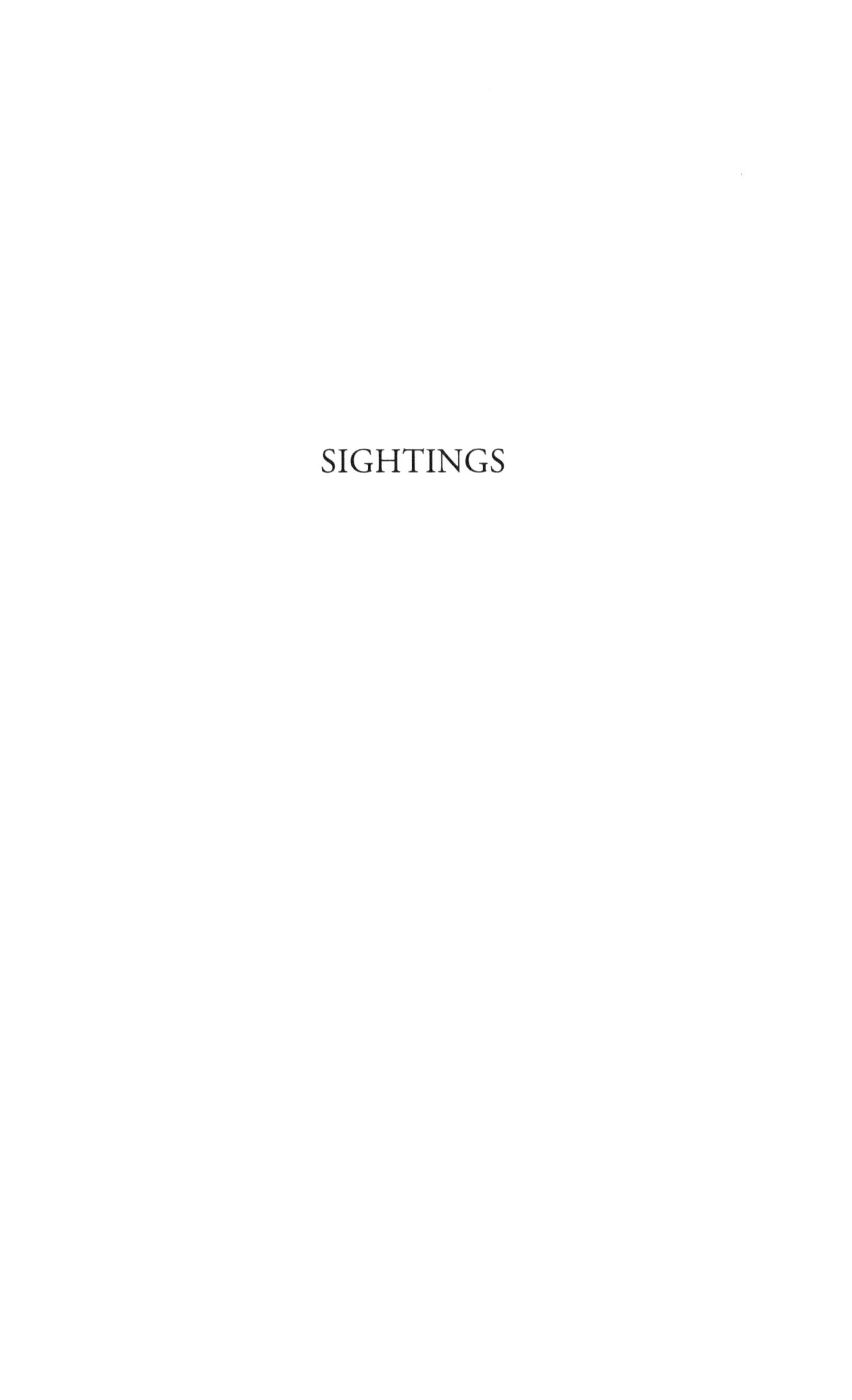

SIGHTINGS

A Chamber of Wonders

Steeled in austral grays,
granite, waterfall, crag, ice floe
imprint on the cold mirror of solitude.

No one was meant to share in this.
The cog and wheel of color,
time's breathing stopped
in a final gasp, an intake of oblivion.

Insignificant intruder
taken off the clock,
I want to go on forever listening
to what craters listen to,
nature's mute momentum.

The glaciers crack and tumble
in a shout of silence.
A puzzle of forest lies between salt tides,
the mountains' silver drool,
grieving evergreens
ghost-hung and meditating.

Phantoms performing at a dance,
that none else came to,
conceal a chamber of wonders
that defrauded polar rules
with the heart of an emerald
bleeding into diaphanous
pools of sorcery.

Moss weeps, sings, claws
its way along rock, bark,
into a likeness of Spring
turning out rainbows.

Who invented this hoarding
of moisture, root maze, bacilli?
Was it accident relayed by opportunity
or a wish carried in by chance?

Kamchatka

Under a squamous sky abruptly tempered
ash-capped cones hold in their bellies.
A pure spirit vaporizes
the serried birches beside bucketing rivers
swum and drunk by coy bards.
In the flat meadows, invisibly,
it opens its limpid eyes.

Bear carries wind on his back
gorging on season, feasting on daylight
claws under water hooking
fish turned cursive and fleet.
Behind the forest line, crystallized
by unchartered distance and time
a huntress borrows illusion
to foreshadow the death of her prey.

Over the bogs and tundra, stars
leave a metallic smell and in pools
the bort of their brilliance.
Pemphigoid pots of mud, hills
grimed with tufa and snow, greens
rolled out between boskets, simulate
golf courses that felt no player's foot,
only a sapience from above and below.
Sigmoid streams in bandit tattoos,
as waving pennants on a spaceship.

Mineral cathedral vaulted
with cloud Simorgs and rainbows.
Every alphabet pregnant with meaning
has borne here its ultimate message.

Plateau

Eyes open, the dead
lay in burial rings
                    of stone and frost

in long blades of silence

conversing with sun-fractured rivers
                            that gurgle over rolled marbles

quenching eons of thirst and

conveying memories
                            to the pervious dream
of the long-distance traveler,

a high princess congealed
                            in her cradle of permafrost,

her vigil long started
                    beneath the eagle's spun shadow

            in the still vortex
            of her unblinking patience.

High on the summits
abiding by ice tabernacles

enigma immaculate with snow

is kept
        by the leopard's discerning footfall.

Four nomad nations sing with voices
of horse hair and fiddle,

assembled in the hallowed meadow

of this ground undisturbed,

they shape mountains and streams,

bend distance into memory.

While a lake winnowed by space,
beats a tattoo of altitude and wind

wordless forthright.

Old Mother

An ancient white lily
with coronets of gold
on a dog-barking street
where bundles of wood
lean bucolic
against city housing,
in a whim of excess
soul-scented her innards
to host her saintly gathering.

Penitents kneel
under windows ambered
by winter's lingering spell.
What miracles of faith are accomplished
by that pale yellow sun!

A draft of invocations
quickens shores of candle light
and iconic eyes moisten.

Oh church of the Arbat, seat of splendors past,
once a forest quaint with countless dryads,
the last four trees in the courtyard
are now banisters of a staircase
to empyrean heights.

Momentary Death

Along the smoky ice of the Neva
the frost-plated trees stand to attention
and the salmon sunset struggles against barriers of gray
unable to dissolve the shadows at palatial moldings.
The city is a dark print of itself.
A black lace of roofs and domes rims the blankness of dusk.
The mystery of oneself has become senseless,
lost to a baleful grandeur that has no innards,
left beside the frozen river like a reptile's skin.
The words come but the heart no longer pounds
for the conjunction of small clues and
private heresies.
The vigor of enigma has gone cold:
the steeples and the cupolas are insolubly trivial.
Between psalm and a shrug
the city is pasted on the outside of the mind.
Walking in sub zero past scattered headlights
- blandly adding their mechanical caution -
is to wander neither to nor from anywhere.

After the Ice Age

Over the flat fields of the north
wind whistles to itself
like a boy with his dog.

Peacock apple trees fan out,
dizzy with the shadows
of their fermenting burden.

Brooks flush out silver bream
tracing halos around
tousled grazers of fire.

Mown hay fields are laid out
for man to spread himself
thin between earth and sky.

Steep, shaggy houses pause to reflect,
en-shrining loneliness along
a gashed and gushing coastline.

Polyvalent cloud curds
devour each other, drool
over a sea big with titans.

Quietly in culverts of grass
man chooses to be
at the center or aside.

A Place in Sweden

Someone has sat here
        Under the eaves
        Waiting,
Feeling that the waiting
Was almost living a constant childhood.
Someone has run delighting fingers
Over the nearly jagged stone wall
Where the square four-paned window,
        Deeply-set like a bird in a tree trunk,
Splashes the sun's morning milk
Over objects vertiginously few.
Space hollowed by the openness
Of fields redundant with daisies,
Of passing puffs:
        A chessboard of absence.
Yet all is there
        Sealed against terror.
The black Gustavian desk enraptured
With its chestnut chair,
The bare wood floor feigning to be a deck,
On which lightly flutters
The white muslin of the bed
Adorned in brass
        Like a Tibetan bride.
The chair listens,
        Listens to everything unsaid.

Books stacked to one side of the desk
        Bound lovingly in leather,
Mark prescriptions for a time
That may yet come.
Spelled out promises burst from their bindings
Revealing the merits of the flaxen room.

Sandham

Some time in the Spring
the shores remain cool,
the water melting through,
the surface candy smooth
with shards of ice beneath,
the ocean so transparent
it prevails as idea.
By the coast the sea is a plate
of crystal, granite, silver.
Lighthouses stand
in stern figments of safety.
The black mantle of pines
casts shadows of disbelief over
the sunny pebbled crescents
where babies now scrape their bottoms
as Vikings once their long-boats.
Boulders step into the deep
as heart beats of conquest,
the hero's dis-guarded toys.
Trees draw the midday rays
in rosettes to their bark.
Stone polished to a mirror
signals to migrating ducks
scooping cloudlets out of their way.
Their explicit path cuts blue ruts northward
to the tundra line
chiseled thin like the lips of a Swede.

Evening Over the Rooftops

Sky above rooftops pays attention
to the finer outlines of the mind.
The chromatic evening calls on
cupolas and spires.
The tide of change, the curse of doubt go below
where even water cannot make up its mind
to be lake river or sea.
Bicycles roll by with gold-spun heads, skins of wheat.
Dyed in sunset, the chill eyes project
an orange savagery pedaling home
where in white rooms they'll cool back to blue.
Sky above rooftops fills with balsamic calls,
timely chimes, the bassoon voice of bronze,
the sheer idea that wills to be divine:
a masterpiece of harm undone.

Red Velvet in Stockholm

The red velvet of northern latitudes
instills the polar night with
the blood of snow flakes
as they tumble
through a fleece of fog over
evergreens and hardened falls.

A color heaped with blondness
borrowed from peony and rose,
mellow peach under crystal chandeliers,
with a legacy of lace cuffs over
the click clack of a game table.

Accidental luxury at a garret window
half hidden by Spring's pursed leaves
a family ruby on a table
the mirror of fire, the length of a sleeve
where even the wrinkle and fading
stay fresh and playful

with a wish to race reindeer,
to ring bells, to drink platinum
from hills of ice.

Cross Country

Where Finland and Russia embrace
Too frozen to untangle
We haunt each other
Winged and bewitched
By an orbit of silence.

Though snow chills like space
The interval between us
Condenses inevitably.

Like seamstresses at work
Fir and spruce brandish needles
Create a scent of darkness
A tear of shadow that opens
Winter's opaque stare
Of intractable distances

Where chimes a fear
Of losing one another.

Our race melts the frost
Shelters us from the gone by
The subdued, the vanished.

Even as we are stripped down to solitude
By January's raw temper
The things unsaid between us
Perform their own spell.
And the monastery's baptismal glare
In this middle of nowhere
Means nothing to us.

Mirage in Finland

The house has off-season windows.
Helpless, it can neither stare back nor blink,
but glistens emptily, an obsolete compound

risen like an iceberg
from the mist of an endless forest
assailed by the premature Spring
of a callous nature.

Once before, I entered these blond rooms
glazed with frosted sun, and
left them my fear of

the incoming tide of a day's ambiguity,
of night's furtive gestation of matter,
its sudden rending by a wing beat.

Each tree a cold statue
to this clear symbol of loneliness,
the house a cage to intangibles.

It vanishes behind me
melting back into 'once upon a time'
random dream or book returned to a shelf,

a mirage retaken by nature's vacuum,
something of me captured, consumed
by an inconceivable elsewhere.

Swimming at Humlebaek

Between shady oaks
steeply regimented on a slope,
pebble-branded shallows
show pellucid,
emitting their freshest purpose.
Overhanging foliage
transforms Kattegat sea into a lake
where a boy stands
with water to his calves,
contemplating the ready relief
of the plunge
that will quench summer thirst.
A girl spin jumps
from a docklet
signaling that the afternoon
is on its way.
By groups of twos and fours
youth in ruffled sand
sprawl before immersion.
A pewter shiver shakes the trees,
the bathers pin up gold manes,
pull on cotton sweaters,
run to bleached houses between the oaks,
to china blue and Danish.

Past Utaoset

Utaoset is passing by,
left to its wind-chilled austerity
of heather and rock,
taking him further
than could the meeting of our eyes,
to blue domes
spinning burrs of ice,
keeping him where I can see,
even as I look toward Finse,
a strong figure,
a runner of winter woods,
a face of icicles
beneath a netted cap
holding back his hair.
Freedom pulled us in
and threw us away again.

Utaoset has gone by.
But when the stars come out
he will shiver and
in solitude's labor
he'll grow out of me.

Dragonite

The old streets wrap around Austrian comfort
with the suppleness of young arms and legs.
White linen windows send out a murmuring sonata,
a grieving cello, the streak of a Slav memory
inter-leaved among their notes.
From the embrace of a cobblestone alley slips the music
and that sliver of well-versed recollection
from ones who neglected to depart.
Quaint and formal behind a bleary window
Biedermeier still sells
bronze looped frames, blue gold studded cups
and a taste for waltzing
poured into cherry red glasses
cut to be the Sunday best of a rich aunt.
Spring shimmers with fairy tales
for those besotted with magic
like the boy throwing a line, or
the old man crumbling along the walkway.
The pavement gleams and slips
under the storm's cave breath.
By the river's dimpled hide young leaves shudder.
Already a bit of summer under the chestnut trees
greets a thousand kisses
in their shadowed shelter
by a dragon spellbound.
The glee and tender fear cast
there by his emblematic vigil!

Stung by Moonlight

Tonight the gentle Elbe
exhales the vulpine scent of woods,
running dark, star gazing.

To reach the north it rises to
the crotchet air of wings
speeding toward the sea
swiveling in galactic eddies
spinning out in waltzes.

Mist embalms the lanterns
in a costumed yellow haze
from centuries long past
along embankment gardens
where a blackbird. inaugurates Spring.

The river loosens a mane
of fog on the streets of Dresden
unflinchingly quaint despite 1945.

On palace, cathedral, opera house
stone statues turn back to flesh,
simulating the March momentum
of buds soon to burst out green
from the cocoon of stilted bark.

Baroque bay windows lean out
over cobblestones fracturing
dressy crystal chandeliers.

The moon swells towards its term
re-shaping chimney stacks and domes
with every flamboyant trick it owns,
engraving itself in nooks and crannies
inking afterhours with spectral calligraphy.

The cold lunar burn
consumes castle windows
whose oval eyes draw me
to take a leap of faith

and test their charry darkness
with my own uneasy fortune.
For tonight the charm of lunacy
has ravished me whole.

The Saxon Engineer

How long this man has fed on next to nothing,
Keeping his feelings in the ice of fortitude,
From when rain in his boyhood repeated
The faulty mantra of a leaky faucet
During all the gray days of his youth.

And iron curtain windows spied
On his two room housing in which season
Upon season faltered and rusted into
Sorrow, stifle, gloom, scowl.

Years later on the fast track of a train
Past exuberant fields and prescient hills
That foresaw the return of the Saxon ways,
He still bows the submissive head
Of a beaten dog, a dying dove.

Forehead post-scripted by a perpetual sentence,
Old memories stalling the machinery
Of his well-made mind.
His wistful eyes suddenly open up
To the workings of seduction.

He remembers when so little was possible
And the heart was brought to heel
Before this woman's time with whom time quickens
As they speed on together at 130 miles an hour.

Lithuanian Transposition

October morning of stainless steel
encircling a kernel of chimes
and silk pleated blinds.

The outer city stiffens under
the boot of a Russian ghost.

Like you.

Buses swarm and swirl around
the station in silver schools.
Beside muscled statues sidewalk trees
look gaunt.
Buildings angular and
stubborn on the outside
cultivate inner contradictions.

Like you.

Beyond a brandished fist far woods
conceal a vermillion fox
tip-toeing across the high octave
of savagery and coyness.

Like you.

Over there a couple waits
for a bus and the morning could be theirs
had the man not looked like you,

that same Stakhanovite shape,
that covert craving mouth.

Like you.

His girl keeps guard yet
he wants me to give a sign.

So like you.

The illicit script
takes him one way, me another

until wishes or fate
bring us back together:

brick castle on swan lake
under a deferred copper sun.

Like you.

Passing Through Venice

The air tastes of milk.
The gaping June sky is
an infant duke yawning.

Under an awning's ambry shade
shimmer brocades of light.
I reverently curtsey to the sway
of clerical pompons.

Trailed by the festive wake of a *Sandolo*
my absent mind floats in the lactation
of noon's sluggish haze.

I too, masterpiece of subsisting
without thought, time or compass.

Above me a *nobile* terrace
pillared with jasmine
has lanterns for night time
so the crescent moon can rest.

Behind that grand front room
there is likely to be
an American lady napping
under a Tiepolo ceiling

while her cat reclines outside
striped in orange splendor
paws pulsing in lazy decrees
over the edge of a green cushion
surveying the watery glaze
of the incoming tide.

Recalling me from elsewhere
the well-heeled puss extends
a greeting with a worldly stretch.

A butler brings him a snack.

Cannaregio

We cross the ghetto square
quartered by light and shadow
tropes of Sunday qualm
on the verge of spirit
or madness seeping
through Chirico's eye.

Like gondolas Jews glide by
glossed over in black.
God's Word flares up
at a synagogue's panes.
Behind patchwork houses
in disguise trickle trickle
fountains of arcana
in tabernacle courtyards
flapping with laundry and wings.
We count the windows
each casting a spell.

A bridge slopes into a comeback.
Santa Maria dell' Orto's hangar
hangs Tintoretto in the dark.
Orchards resurrect
in the hale alpine air
mellowing noon's garden
with yellow pears.

Under a rickety passageway
a sepia wonderland.
Centuries wrote their epitaphs
on the beaten-up wall
of a factory or a palace.
Three canals converge south
where alchemy transmutes
water into treasure.

On Schiavone's beach
we hear the stampede
of vesper bells
at crepuscule.
On the incendiary stage
gilded paragons
atop their domes change
back into daredevils.

On to Itself

Once more the Doge's palace blinks
At the sunset with frothed eyelids.
Once more San Marco performs
The day's closing ritual
And San Giorgio's sky fills
With flamboyant specters
Flaunting the intimacy
Between things and nothing
Tangible or unfathomable.
Night is about to extinguish
All the crepuscular reds
That adroitly combine
Fires lustful and hallowed.
The eye stares to frame the picture
Before it fades out.

Hermaphrodite bells
Chime to themselves.
Vaulting seagulls draw
Unperceived graphs of emptiness.
Venice suddenly left to itself
Plies its lonely prodigality
To the four elements of which
I've become the alien,
Singularly inhuman,
Drained of marrow and warmth,
Senses outperformed by another

From the fourth or eleventh dimension.
I pace in a realm revealed
In the gap between wake and slumber,
Exhaling my own distortion
In a city purged of flesh
Where vapors wrap dereliction
In celestial ivy
Around stone balconies.
Scabbed walls sinking back
In the mud from which grew
This scheme of splendor
Recount a love for which
There is no form or measure.
Solitary footsteps resound
Up through wind and stars
To the other city.

Basilica

Penumbra committed the marble
to the murky shades of the sea
in this church of domes where
the mist-washed blue sky at its windows
in daylight recalls some disposition
of the city's midnight, draping
its profligate gloom about the aisles.
In mineral obscurity the statues of saints
amidst battalions of candles,
count those that are lit
and soften their stiff robes
in the pliant glow of wax,
projecting pleas of unexpected innocence
at their solemn hems,
each flame a beacon
watched from misery's perch
around which watery darkness
hoards untried delights.

Venetian Winter

Under the arcades lanterns hang like bombs
suspended between ignition and extinction.
At the shadow-line a cat wanders
and the passerby wonders:
what is here for me?

The grand mid-floor living rooms
turn on their evening assets,
grow formal hearts of glass
in cold imitation of the spangled Grand Canal.
The city drifts through the chill like a forlorn lover.

The adorning vapor follows the churning boat.
A glimpse of ornate beams, a shaded bulb shining
off a frame, a bowl of puffy peonies
leave darkness unresolved. A cocktail shaker
chugs back into thc dusky stream.

Murderously pale, a light ascends
a courtyard staircase casting a spell of crime.
Where is the flowered hair, sweetness on the stone ramp?
Phosphorescent, the fawn grins savagely back.

The stripped arms of a tree racked
across a gunpowder sky
make a lonely appeal
and a chronic nostalgia rations the windows
that emerge from the night.

Loire

One doubts aging
Moments do not singe
But hover in lustrous permanence
Translating the dark green
Of a taste of storm
Even under the sun's scepter
One doubts getting older
Under the charm of romance
Out-spoken
On the cloud opiated turrets
Of a Tuffeau stone castle
Lucent with windows and carvings
Glittering back at the river
That shapes mirages of islets
Asleep on beds of sand
Vineyards liquored with evening gold
Pastures slipping into formal gardens
In which each flower is word to a thought
Dahlia and rose pentacles made
To ride the bubbling boxwood
Prismatic fountains titling chapters
Read both from earth and above
The river barters chests of sunlight
For Perrault fables
Seated at the open window
Leafy shade capers
Drawing fairylands on paper

The damask of an armchair
Deepened into a copse conceals
A girl, a beast, a hag......dusk
Lingers on the white casements
Leaving the rooftop chimneys
Entangled with twilight.
Summer trees grow tall
Rooted in monarchy.

Pays Basque

The Rhune mountain
cast the house down below
in a mid-summer's play
where we acted out
a trance from before our time
on the fogged lawns
of proto-history.

To our doorstep came
an Infanta in green.
Inside our white walls
crossed like crusaders
by red painted beams
one or another of us
became for the others
providence magus unicorn
spelled inside the vellum
of an illuminated script.

By day tidy linen drew sun
to our fingers in heaps of gold.
At night like pet cats we settled
near starched armoires.

The metamorphic peaks
angled for our souls
drunk on the incense
of waxed furniture.

When the Rhune came down
with howling cloud chasms
leaching lodes of ore
we sat within reach
of each other
nearly outside
spellbound by opened doors
as it poured almost cold
relieving us of heat
tuning us to the wind
nearly abducting us.

Summer Storm

The hour contrives a fragrance
of laurel and alpine water.

A baby follows with kitten eyes
the liede of rain on his cowry skin.

Then heavy drops thud in Iron Age rituals.
At windows geraniums blow kisses

to the gusty surge of trees
where turbulent shadows build

dungeons, unearth crypts
bind the dragon to the cloud

in a story that is retold
for no other purpose than

the mother, daughter, child
keeping their immutable vigil of love.

Mother has chiseled auburn hair
invincible Ptolemaic features.

Under the dark voluptuous foliage
daughter blazes like a harvest.

Magi infant waves his arms
spell-binding the black lake

monogrammed with swans before
the mineral decrees of teatime

on thick rugs where the old
continent long made itself at home

and charm bracelets jingle across
the table like gold dockets of magic.

Antiquity

Pines black with evening
return to this same hour
ever shadows of themselves
in Odyssey's lengthening twilight.

Artful immortality devises a language
common to the still ether of Olympus
and the tempo of the cicada.

The long-necked pines take off
in flocks from the cliff
in tandem with the cormorants.

The cove uncovers depths of transparency
wise with lucid flashes from
mullet schools that foresee
a kingfisher's dive.

Acrobatic swallows sharpen the air
slicing out paths
between above and below.

Sounding, then anchoring,
pirate winds quiet down
and dissolve in the Circean haven.

Back to Versailles

Blue door nests in a wall
be-draggled by extraneous roots
and scavenger moss,
outlawed gate to the foothills of history,
though a few may yet trespass.

An alley paces between box hedges
in a frock coat, cracking a whip
against the prophetic wall distressed
by a conflict of forces.

Rain falls on the brink of a spell
collects into clumps of flowers.
Grounded weeds bedew with prayer.

The path disappears into a posthumous dusk,
a mountainous wreckage of ivy,
topsy-turvy fairytale spilling home truths.

A sudden benevolence stokes the sodden day.
The sun plays harpsichord
and grooms the park with light.

Now, a blue silk flag waves you in.
The weald and the field wear ribbons of mist
and play shepherd to sundering clouds.

At St David's

Hyperopia of rock-hard coastline
To nacre and gold leaf horizon
Dedicated to a smuggler's dream of bounty
In the spray of dolphin leaps,
Odyssean seals fed on umbilical algae.

Sheared lining of ancient land and unfledged wave
Tailored by the seagull's speculative glide.
Prey-eyed sheep in spongy parks
Graze on salt shoots of grass
While above drowned seamen
Man their cargo clouds.
Shaggy moor anchored to the tides
Monoliths of silent narratives
Still pulsing to the toll of surf
Slim rain drizzling
Off south Britain's fog.

Bony hill born to brume's mystic plasma
Father to a holy pool where
Once drank the hungry panther.
Cathedral immersed in memory's mist
And the stately decay of virtue.
Winter's end expels a cloud of crows
On an axis of witchcraft.
Naked elm roots fused
To a rift of white whelks and crocuses
Dug by scuppets of season
Branches spin incantations
Weaving shady worship in the sky.

The Forgotten Temple

Far from the scrapes of life,
                    a bald patina

of clayed buffalos deep
              in squelching grooves

made from effort and imprecations
              that is man's common tale

recounted by the million punctuations
                    of round head palms

spawned by a jaundiced sun
                    rapt with a soggy horizon of toil.

Far from this flat rice storage
                    other lives have petrified

except my own possessed
              by abstraction or aberration

from before the Apsara
              their hour-glass gesture

from before
        the trick of history

a temple of python and cobra
looped into foundations

grown out of the motion of trees
chambers revisited

in utmost silence
by monumental spirits.

Entrails of stone
digesting chaos.

I place a bold foot
between apprehension

and oblivion,
to pass the elaborate threshold

where the reign of wilderness
beguiles with a bygone spell.

Over Bangkok

A sheet of glass suspends me
in the sodden air.
A rain dragon stormed in
a fever of wind and mist
to wipe out Bangkok.
I was looking for a different forecast.

A flock of birds flee,
shaving off high cornices.
Tarped long boats, double-deckers
still barter their river fate,
the cable bridge now an unfinished sentence.
Buried in wet chill
contrived by the air con at my back,
all disappears without a fight,
absconded by fog.

Beyond the water lily rug,
the embossed velvet,
I am blind.
Jazz tries to sedate the room.
The wood panels hum
with a spiritual diction.
No evidence of reality.
Where have I gone?

Within the invisible,
inside the Temple of Dawn.

Illumination on the Tatai

Muscled spirits of the jungle night
        Made us faint with darkness
On the thin-hipped deck
        With a baldachin of raffia
Boundless with adventure
        That purled high over the swarthy
Leaf-stamped tressing and wrestling of the river.
        The Cardamoms heavily made up
With Mount Mehru mystery
        Locked us inside perplexity.
In this sandy gullet of savagery
        Proclaiming not far from the sea.
The excitable pulse of romance
        devised a constellated obscurity
Flashing with options
        Life, death and all
That dressed to kill in between.
        Three sister trees blinked
        Up a chatter
        Of tiny fairies in their bows.
The small dexterous hand
        Of the khmer hunter
Picked off Tinks
        That glowed in our expectant palms
Rewarded with magic.

Brought Back

What remains of a shawl
once the wrap of dawn shoulders
of a child goddess or
broad sash wound around the waist
of a boy ordained to rule.

Left on a chair in dire need of a plot.
Curio on display, beauty slighted
by the forces of estrangement.
Ruined rapture, reptile digesting
self of pointless splendor.
A remnant with a death wish.

Say you still belong to tropical penumbra
atrium to the exquisite night
of barefoot mahogany floors
where you first unraveled.
Say you are made of the silvery twine
of rain torrents and drizzles,
of gardenia oil, of a celadon poison
from a bloom-drugged snake,
from the cerulean pool snug in fern,
dyed with vibrissa and fallen feather,
from knotted rainbow threads.

I wish your return to the saffron dust
of wide eastern avenues chiming
with bells of resurrection,
to the gold-leaf layering of entreaty.

You undulate through the room
driven by shadow and sunlight
toward the plea in my skull's stupa.
You slip and slide away from ruin,
black stitching scented with opium,
silk pocket to a star,
river to hot sandbanks of desire,
weaving yourself into my footstep and caress.

Take your chance.

Bay of Invisible Merits

The city heaved, scrambled up
the other flank of the headland.
On its drug-fumed and soiled instep
ruins in black cotton endured,
shoe-string men in shorts spat trotting
under bamboo cages and tin trays,
the agony of their racing tempo
regulated by despotic rackets.

She turned her face another way.
Cliff-hanging trees bristled with jade dragons.
Fruit milk dripped into a soft-spoken sea,
a bay forgotten by the brash sunsets
wrought from melted arm-bands and crowns
once worn by jungle dancers.
Blue-black fresh like a love bruise
Where she and he bathed undaunted,
in the obscure heaven of myth
where swam a slow-wagging shark.

She perspired in diagonals of silk
beneath lanterns hanging from the dark.
Just beyond them she could see
the airy volumes of leafed peristylums,
nymphaeums, tabliniums:
wing-swept cognizant rooms,
instant arcades of consummate grace.

A car tracked vertigo along the corniche:
Two idlers in evening dress
sucking kisses at hairpin turns.
It roused a sense of luxury
and seclusion akin to slumber.
A tremor of breeze spread over the bay
plying the wand of a moon beam,
working the arcane craft of elation.

Yellow Silk

The parable is from imperial days.
Its yellow silk screens the blue sky.

Cool in the dawn mist of the Peak
I read the subtitles of a legendary China,
the rock-veined rondure courtyards
their Coryphee pines in step,
ivory-carved plots,
the alembicated recipes of elaborate pleasures,
heat's squeeze in jungles of metaphors
perspiring the subtle venoms
of wasted wisdom,
camel-back verse powdered with snow,

where the junks glide by on their dark creature wings
through the fretted larynx between Kowloon and Victoria,
extending their bid for serenity
past Cheung Chao towards Lantau.

Now volatile morning slips into
a tropical symphony pairing anticipation
with the vast relaxation of the sea.
Skyscrapers grown from water roots
shimmer below in evaporations of metal and glass
and in their electronic shade pedestrians
open at every stride lilies of the past.

Gray velvet bars snooze like tomcats
at the edge of rush hour, only
waking to night's banquet of cybernetic lights.

In the city's midriff of Period getaways
brown ventilated rooms hide
love affairs, quiet in their lairs
between potted palms and waxed tiled floors
living out archetypes of colonial charm.

And I, bathed in the orchid tide
of a terrace jutting over Hong Kong,
take my watch and breakfast.

At Clark's Pool

Sultry dusk perspires
from the slow making and undoing of life.

Drifting roots bubble into flower,
leaves unfurl and fall in endless substitution.

Nothing shortcuts the everlasting rut
except the chimeras of darkness that slash

at the blundering mess of stars
like blades of abstraction.

Engendered by night's hangings,
brews of blood and air

the bats unpredictably surf
the intangible waves of fate.

Havelock Island

Of the slow chameleon sky
before man's longing for gods
there is little to say.

Save for the un-charted intimacies
between land and sea,
the friction of trees exhaling bird smoke,
the beach flat on its belly,
the spell of the rhythmic wave
over the unquenchable sand
the forest batting lianoid lashes
when lizards dart over root
knuckles and worming limbs,
the muddy jaws of the mangrove
where ocean peeled off
the tide's salty rinds.

Nothing thinks, silence fulfilled.

Then 'far' mutates among the echoes of nature,
drifting in to watch the hatching of solitude.
Dawns begin to hemorrhage,
dusks grow reclusive.
Lush pillars resound and shiver with awe,
lamenting the soft blacker night.

Spirit knows itself as man's
legacy of loneliness.

Fog of the Sundarbans

Carry me fog, float me above the reeling world,
aloft in contemplation. Rain
your slow countdown of dreadful suspense
over where the mangroves still customize
their Paleolithic arches to fit the gaping mugger maws,
white bellies beached on the stench of
rotting rattan and invertebrates.
Where the gray syrup of the delta
fills and bubbles out of crab holes,
leaves an unsuspected gem or two
with every doleful flux over the soggy floor,
bloated and porous like a tea cake,
and mud hoppers scatter like marbles out of a bag.
The soundless flicker of a leap still lights
the wick of nature. Shape of adoration
and disquiet among the coiled and knotted shadows,
the flame wavers through the fog.
Low, the warning slip of the reptilian tongue
may soon recount the last tree on which
tarnished and nostalgic our relapses hang.
The silence, a clamor in a chamber of death
where none will know how to move with ease
but extinction lapping deeper into the waterways.
So carry me, fog, carry me over the sinuous tides,
the industrious budding and falling of leaves, an anguished
fleet of deer until, fluid and vital,
the tiger dawns burning through your dismal shroud.

Lagoon

Lagoon, palimpsest of heaven
on which a thousand lithe visions of sun
come to rest in hallowed epics.
No boat's dark form keeps the mind's compass
from the core of nature:
surf, shimmer, undulation,
glory sung on the white helix of the reef.

Mount Gower

In solitude framed
by the dark grimace
of basalt palisades
and their talus down
to the roughing waves
an old man casts his line.
The ocean tosses back
its own cruelty.

Mocking gravity,
fairy terns hover
at the corner of his eyes.
He is shrunk by
the upward scale of the land
where summits secrete fog,
an envied primacy.

Island upon island riven
by condensation.
Filmy deck of
a nebulous ship.
In the levitating dimension
of the atonal shroud
incubates a symphony.

Moisture opened umbrella ferns
under whose lustrating limbs
bird and plant grown
under the aegis of innocence
masquerade in mist.

In vain the fisherman
longs to surrender
in wonder
to what he cannot tow in.

Far Into the Night

Groves of Kentia palms notch
their fronds with breeze and stars.
Play chamber music to a graveyard
jostled by spirited headstones
where lawn and hibiscus flowers
weave a rug for the sand-filled
footsteps of the beachcombing dead.

Birds emerge from their burrows,
wings akimbo like vampires waking
spread a velvet inquisition through the night,
low-flying shadows spinning off their whims.
Enamored like moths with the garden lantern
of a sky lit from within by sparkling eddies.

Rock prows dip in the foam of the reef,
shaking salt water from their decks.
Along the beaches fish like ponies crowd
the fencing shore in search of treats.

Nature whispers, embraces,
compels with all its arms and kisses
seeking me out with wave lengths.

Polynesian Morning

Indecision before creation
sea and sky still immersed
in each other's reflection.

Intangible horizon veiled in
naught, beyond reach
of the defining hour.

At the combed edge of sand
water melts in a spasm
as if saying 'at last' and
irons out deception.

At the tip of the shoal
invisible footsteps
neither alight nor take off
but to everywhere at once.

A radiance appears where
smelted green and blue
fulfill an alien calm.

The sky catches its breath,
leaks colors and contrast,
complicates everything.

Sea Born

The bow churns a farewell to the dock,
an indolent breeze under the aft awning.
Passengers heaped in a sated daze
of piglet feasts, wilting blossoms,
skin plated with sandalwood oil.

The ship strings a harem of candy isles
striped with mint shade, lemon sand,
wrapped in the silks of ocean and light.

There is nothing to tell the ship
from the man whose far-seeing eyes
washed and re-washed with blue
are those of a Hessian baron
gone astray in latitudes,
big hands quiet with past fights.

Through the dark scales of the Tongan trench
sharks pencil in their fins.
The scrolled native lips of the sailor
part as he watches, deep,
the bubbly wake of whales
the spray of three spouts
like the birth of new islands
seldom noted in the sclera of distance.

Land of Men (*Fenua enata*)

Be as tall as these islands that plunge
straight into the ocean at their feet.
Stretch, sway, glisten like the sea
in the star-spiked evening
before the night's black mountain of silence.
Listen to the oracle organs that tentacle
with foam into the earth's smarting heart.
Do it, for a new frontier
is to be reached and
the reasoning of these islands is best.
Enchantment here not undone
by roar, complaint, cruelty,
inexplicable loss. It is
benevolence pervading
the driving swells and
tying umbilical cords
between currents and sky.

To spite their sullen rock sentinels,
valleys open operatic fans,
spend the hard earnings of love.
Down from shattered clouds shimmer
white terns penning their sunlit verse
across green-tiered cliffs.
Read it again.

When did stone and tree
pretend to be harbingers of heaven or hell?
When did the voice of mystery
become artistry
and when did the idle child
demand a destiny?
When did the anxious mind
initiate a war between itself and nature
to impose its own lineage?
Ponder this when
the cormorant hops away
from the sucking rolls so
like a frightened priest.

Through Rain

Sobs of gray water
rain down on China.
Towns like dirty aprons
are tied to ashen rice fields
under the obstructed sky.

Fog and the wear of revolution
have settled on this June evening.
Thoughts overflow
the tracks leading
from Shanghai to Beijing.

The sharp tide of reverie
draws its sword
across the uniforms of industry,
rubble and high brick walls
tangled with rusted wire.

In the deception of speed,
a contorted pine at dusk
shelters black-necked geese
in recondite shadows,
returns them home
along silver-tuned canals.

In the darkness
of China's eastern provinces,
phantom eyes wink
through a slanted downpour,
at shuddering panes.

May in Shanghai

Perpendicular to the Bund's strand
Side streets pull on their oars up the river
Refreshing their old film make-up
Printing colored postcards of themselves
With a hungry nostalgia and boutiques.

Arctic air hollows through revolving doors
With a satiated purr cooling
The pelt of the Shanghai beast.
Flash of a deep blue flank.
A Jag sidles up to the curb.

A kitten slums on his store stoop
Whines that its time to close
To his mistress immersed
In the sales price tagging
Of her celadon china.

An alley wires black crow's feet
Across a dented and smoggy sky
Yet abandoned the ritual hanging
Of bleached underwear,
Those streamers of the past.

Pale green, a muslin dress
Undulates on a satin hanger
With a manta ray's heavy grace
Awaits the grand occasion
An inauguration, a love confession.

Waldorf Astoria whispers in onyx shade
Wearing the ladyship tiaras of chandeliers.
The garden made jungle where starched
Table cloths gleam like moonlit pools
Begonias emerge from hedges like painted natives.

Employees rush before the evening downpour.
Rain already smells of the promise
That daytime will be rinsed off.
Sudden puddles splash in electric hues
And city man drinks at his artificial springs.

The Sanctuary

I drifted into the Forbidden City
on a vapor of tadpoles and rusted pipes
that rose from the moat.
A student turned to smile,
teeth like wet pebbles.
Swallows swam above
in the blue nets of summer,
gullets jammed with pellucid *odonata*.
Thrones bore solitude
like shackled wizards
as Orlando shrews
imagined emblemed silks
on their broad behinds.

By the Hall of Terrestrial Tranquility,
under an umbrella pine
I saw the emperor, still young
on a satin swing
sway to and fro,
three empresses by his side:
one slim and moist like a papyrus stem;
the other two powdered with gold
like Mallard ducks,
jade baubles in their ears,
lapis lazuli sprigs in their hair.

‘This place has preserved its ghosts’,
I observed, ‘such immeasurable pollution’.
In cool shadows I watched
the emperor’s endless oscillations
and objected ‘Why so constantly?’
‘All will die if I stop’
said the son of Heaven.
From his robes
rituals soared among the swallows.
At Wumen gate
though the cannon boomed,
I saw imperial kites.

Portrait of Myself as Gong li

Red the suit, red the lips,
wanton Morse of stilettos,
black cinematic umbrella.

Streets deep as forest, dark with plots
lit by neon, deserted by birds
that took off on the slim goodbye of a flute.

The Bund drips with silver threads
from a Lanvin gown. Windows throw
a sheen of pennies onto the asphalt below.

The hidden moon of a storm slides
by the plasma of the Huangpu,
retiring like a distant relative.

Close by, leguminous skyscrapers
shoot up, calling down space
to fashion another dimension.

Under the achromatic spell
she is born of an old-fashioned
felony, itself born from a Guzheng.

She is molded, cinched by rain
and fumes, in urban ecstasy
with no further to contemplate.

Flute Forest at Qing Cheng

Families expelled on weekends
by their over-wrought city
seek refuge in satin China where

the mountain bellows ignite nostalgia,
their mystery offered
for an entrance fee.

A vegetal emulsion sweats luscious
over the strata of an ancient sea
overlooked by butterflies and bees,

their steep forest perspiring
into the bowl of a lake, round
reptilian eye of a dragon,

his tears falling in specters
here then there from rock
to rock cloaked in moss.

A bamboo thicket crosses swords
with silence and manufactures
a flute that soars upward

to the solitude it may catch,
taking pilgrims high
on the black aroma of cypress,

in palanquins of intuition
towards the lofty wisdom
of a Confucian epigram.

One man of many trudges
up the slope on rutted legs,
bent by life's rehearsals.

At each step taken
he gives thanks for the gift
of his hard bare feet

as the flute plays him
many versions of himself
that climbed here before

Mineral Market

Ossified fingers
hoard bits of value
once by decree outlawed
labeled now defiantly
luck, freedom, grace
which was all one to those
who'd lost much of their hope
for life's rewards. Now

they surround morsels of coral,
crags of jade, pearl raiment,
carried on rapids and reptiles
of gold. Their over-worked hands
delivered from factory lines

scrounge through trunks full
of primeval mutations.
From these treasure heaps
tradition returns with
a baton to lead overtures

composed of red reef clots:
the fairy flesh of mermaids,
lashings of dragon tails:
the green liturgy of caves,
the ring of sliding bangles.

The People crouch on frayed shadows
and with talons of age
grab, knot, cup and weigh
the old emblems of worth
against their sum of wizened souls.

Beneath livid light
lost expectations return.
Stone grows anatomies
coral branches into veins.
All organs of well-being.

In a bag of goodies
they take home a faith
in folklore and one
auspicious mineral
will be placed on an altar.

Rice Culture

The stack shelved rice paddies
pull out their harvest drawers.
Clouds channel into open veins
seep downward from shallow to shallow.
A cone hat figure with mud slick fingers
draws a blissful bent solitude
where once the forest grew.
Monolithic buffalo, one palm tree,
hijack the man's aloneness.
Early stars light up
at his wet ankles like fireflies.
What's left of the jungle is
a soft reprimand,
a green valley darkness below
where the water runs fullest.
One day in a roar, this man-made nature
will be taken back.
From across the sea another island
still free of renunciation
will return to the muted shores
the glory of ancient gods.

I too pray to revisit
this plotted landscape
when the punctual call of the scimitar
has ceased to slash the gentle twilight.

Coal Picking

He is busiest of all
working over time
at some jest of living.

My unforeseen love of humanity
is just now born
of this little old fellow
at Ghumi's toy train station.
No doubt a sign
that I am nearer to heaven

cloud pillows at my feet
my gaze floats over
this vestige of man
that lends me halo and wings.

Wizened hands flutter
between the tracks
like leaves blown about
at season's end.

He never looks up
knowing the schedule
by dint of a daily routine.

Master of self-interest
-karma be damned-
chemist of misery's formula
trowel scooping gravel
sorting out free morsels of coal
distantly subsidized
by Darjeeling Himalayan Railway.

Inside the shambled poetics
of his shack above the line
dug out of the Dhupee forest
and a bank of fog
another evening is rescued
by the glow of a scanty harvest
where in reprieve he stares.

Beware that though
some sameness in us both
condenses and evaporates
into the mirage of altitudes
coronated with mist
and gods he is
far busier than me
with no time for pity.

Padparadscha

Marvel of a recalcitrant Spring
cool with fog and the intention
of great heights cowling
their labor of conception even while
on the drumlins tidied in tea rows
affects a more immediate creation.
Blindfolded eyes turn away
from the blue memory of glaciers
though they crack and tilt there
in constant metamorphosis
through quiet accumulation
and the ice sizzle of revelation.
Blossoms appear through
the undulant disbelieved flannel
more mirage than substance
texture and breath untouchable
except by the seer rose
infinitely pastel in its elfin temple
of leafage – algid fantasy dreamt
by the tumid tropics far below.
In a dining-room a woman's
mimosa and pink sari re-calls
the soft yolk and blood
of buds, fulfilling her
with a sense of apotheosis.

Cutting through the mist
the roses crystallize as if
to deny their pliancy
and display their many
facets sparkling now in a heap
of Padparadscha gems.

The Puzzle

The way to Darjeeling tells
A chaplet of burgs hung
Between reams of greenery
Piled high on both sides
As offering to bodhi's altar.
What for, Darjeeling?

On bold terracing
Singled out trees
Domed out of sight
By birds' treble
Discipline the monsoon's
Diarrheal mudslides.

Card castle built on air and faith
Darjeeling juts a stubborn chin
Of embellished pediments
Over a world below
Not forgotten though
Looked down upon.

People tight rope and abseil
Between steam train and the exposed
From irreverence to sublimity.

Fog creeps and nestles
Against cottage window sills
Colonized by potted Gentians.

Near-sighted streets
Darted with roses
Bundle up, infused with the brown
Of coal fires, brewing tea,
Pashmina shawls, stray dogs,
Roof prowling macaques,
Faces square and tarred
By manliness and
The uniformed bustle
Of fluted lapels
Among a bunching of cars.
Ribboned braids, blood red lips
In the haze recall
A Hogarthian England.

There in vaulted gangways
A compound is bottled
Both cozy and sly
Of this urban puzzle
In which magic claims
Its golden due
Of menace and charm.

Prairie

In this pan of fallow grass
is a luck that must be seized

a sudden lifting of crates of life
piled high in stuffy places.

The prairie breathes with the knockout muscle
of an American buffalo

resting alone in a space of animal seity
a terrene force
born of the flaxen ripple

once a blue and reflective sea
in a likeness of the sky
millions of operatic years ago.

By a stream hemmed with acacia,
a trim of green partially bars
his snub profile with a pensive air

while snakes swim through the meadow
sea jewels of the mind
looping sacred knots.

Hill after hill, pastures and herds
gently stamp the signets
of some vast peace treaty.

At a diner, an auburn-haired man
with a dancer's stance and carved out cheeks
smiles a kiss with the same uncluttered candor.

A Favorable Moon

The ferry slices moonlight
in night's flavor of departure.
Clouds hover and coax
the cool-eyed stars to approach.
The free hand of far away
draws flotillas of longing
for clown fish lagoons

while the wind of journey
and a favorable moon
buffet and disembody me.
The bleached highway
shaped from ocean
has an adagio heart
on and on of serenity.

A passenger ship bright
with glow worm chemistry,
departs with bits of Boston
in its portholes
onto the open range
of running wishes
the city left behind
dimmed by nostalgia.

An island in profile
displays lonely bravura but
something too of the wilderness
that once defied settlers.
It still claims a savage due
over this patchwork continent.

Posada of Creeping Horror

Iron bed. Yellow walls
painted with lemon grass, a horse hair brush.
Virgin Mary of placid brow
enameled and central
like a train station, a throbbing heart.

Leafy chisel of lead candlesticks
made for a girl's first communion.
Bathroom robed in Roman grandness
of white and grey marble.
In those afternoon shadows
is a church aisle desperate
with a lover's fervor
competing with utopic hedges of
blue-blossomed Spring outside.
The French lure of a wood desk
nostalgic for the provincial charm
of a crystal carafe shaped for perfume
even as it shivers like the moonstone river
of night's remotest lights. Two cut-glass
tumblers beached on a silver tray
toast a respite from the Indian haired pampa.
Europe nods and preens from wall to wall…

A monstrous thing from hell
scabbed like a knee wound
totters across the bedspread,
turns cunning antennas toward
the Virgin's forgiving features.
By Diego's swift hand
the demon is brushed off the bed
and thrown into the abyss of a sewer.

From a Balcony Over Sarmiento Street

A car screeches by
the grace of Spring
for the seasonal sweetness
of its protracted kiss
beneath the plane trees
laden with the dust
of pipe exhaust.

One might just die
from the splendor of a bird's
crystal gong born
on the evening quiet
along pastry-colored houses.

The streets light up and corner
their prayers so that time
at last will cease.
Look then!
The cupolas bulge with delicacies
in the twilight,
revelations drop into
the deep lap of wishing.
Trees grow through the walls
into upper rooms
in whose Hesperian calm
old ones, given to embellishment,
rest happy with the fragrance
of many Springs before.

Young poor mother
walks by, thin,
as pliant as a reed,
as beautiful as no one knows how,
pushing her baby through
the city's belated silence.

No Speeding

The near-sighted uplands of Santa Cruz
forget the ocean below
repudiated
by an inner lair of silence and mist.
Evaporations of solitude
cabled by silver tendrils
shiver through trees
re-shaped into bones.
A mossy stillness heralds rain.
Clouds drape over
inarticulate instinct
nesting over impulses
in the pleats and
buttonholes of survival.
Giant saddle back turtles
domed with introspection
burdened with keratin helmets,
totter darkly
on scaled amphibian stumps
through green tunnels
of rumination
on a slow descent
to coastal feeding.

The surveillance cameras
of their slanted eyes
scan this and that
with dawning perspicacity
rediscover the vague outline
of memory and time
along a paved bicycle path
their slow-motion scrape
saddened
by cars speeding by
on the main drag.

There Is Good in That Devil

Your face turns to me
quickening,
prelude to a *zarzuela*.
Your face is a sun god
to a Rodriguez or a Falla.
A carnation dusk
peppered with reluctant desire.
The plaza nauseated
with ordinary tourism
surveys your lean stride
and the short raincoat stressing
its smart English stutter.
In that high Inca air you flow,
the thinner of the two,
the felonious pedigree
of your cheekbones
a curse on the sour churches
livid with bleeding bodies
and dolled up madonnas
on the Plaza de Armas,
a plague on all catechisms
a praise of disobedience.

You hunger for altitudes.
Colossal stones pile up
along your path, subdued,
clinched together with enigma.
Topaz steppes run before
the spread wings of the Andes.
A breathless world cleft into chasms
garbed in tumescent forest
bearded with nature's afterthought
hails your insolence,
grows flowers refulgent
with the hue and scent
of this alternative campaign
constellated with paradox,
born of an odd kindness
open-armed with unlikelihood.
There among garish butterflies
the ruthless seduction
of a velvet horned moth.

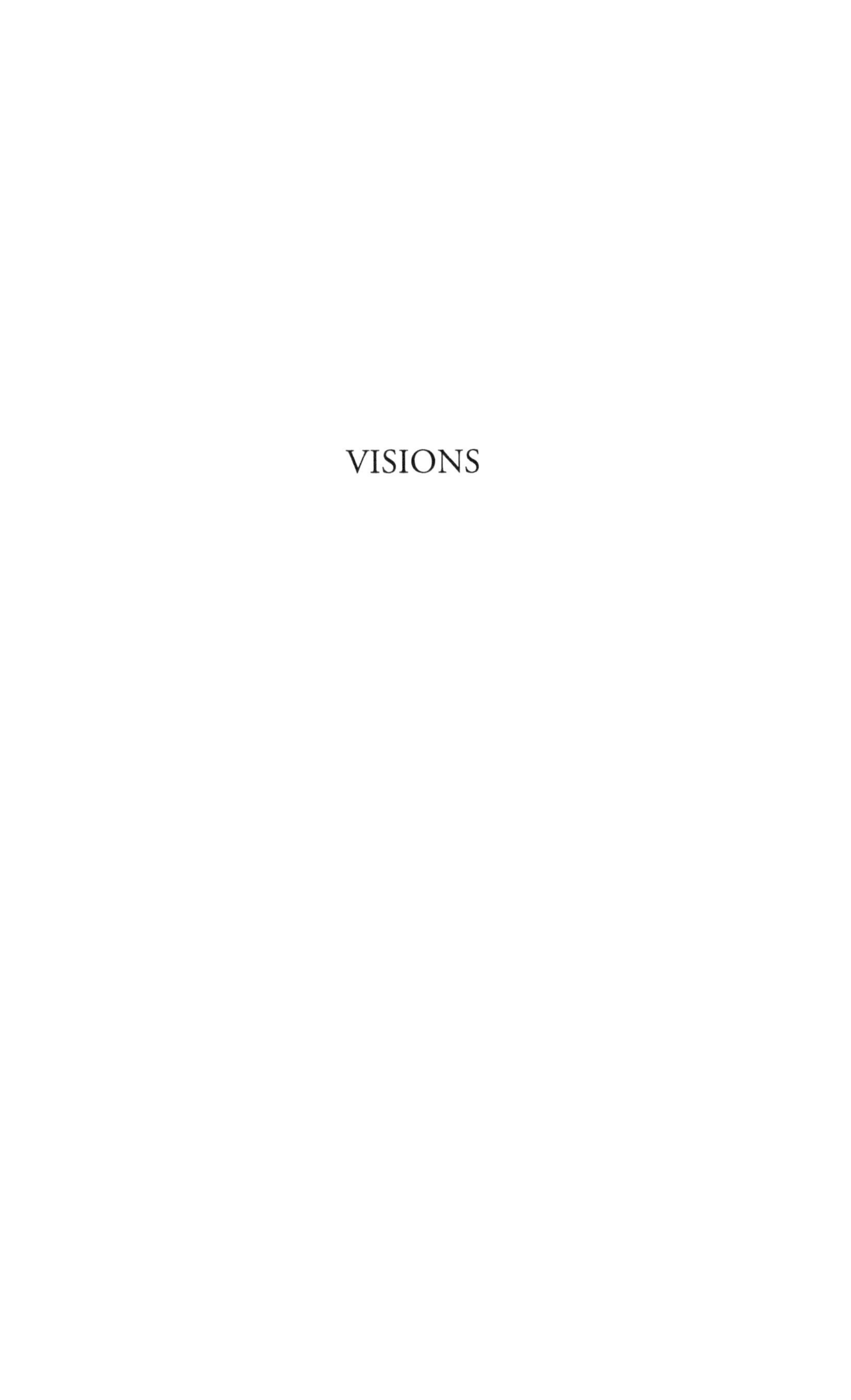

VISIONS

Bear River

A line is drawn there against the business of man.
The frowning spruce watch over mercurial greens
where the bay breeds a full-bodied river to a libertarian sea.
In the inkpots of the creek behind, autumn spends freely,
tossing gold coins afloat with blithe buoyancy.
Carmine maples gather close to the water
rooted in spiraling eddies, portals
to endless spinning yarns
where man has so small a part
and hybrid bodies of rock and tide
born to sensation hide far from the irrelevant sun
that keeps the deerskin hunter square-shouldered
among his provident trees though he cannot perceive
the parallel monologues that speak his absence
over the wave-rutted beach haunted by
fossilized breath and propulsion, tumbled jasper,
calcium turbines and abandoned stairwells.
Silence always a gulping of space,
a transparency in which hoariness reunites with youth
and secrets blown apart diffuse
their ciphers back into the pervasive hush.

Back Home Under the Sky

The road proceeds on past
a desert bulged with sky
that long ago took refuge
from the monotonous asphalt line
in a parallel compass.
I too repeat the enigma of myself,
disabled by this dry snub,
seeing ahead but a planet
of other places.
But when scarlet sunset nests
over the yucca fields,
when antelope blood whittles out
archaic profiles, totemic sentinels
on the filmogenic mesas
then, in that distance of myself,
I try, with pickets of wonder,
to fence in the mirage
of a bare rider on a pinto gliding
into ancestry's magenta realm
without snort or stumble
over sage and rubber rabbit brush
into a scrimmage of silences.
His colors do not match
the monochrome of my history.
The valley's sand-aproned monuments
glorified by the sun's last flare
chisel and shelter his memory.

Under shadow cantilevers
extended by the crags,
there, his grand-mother's tomb
the hare marked with a leap,
just as that Navaho canters by.
Among hallucinating herbs he rests.
Darkness spills kegs of stars and breeze
over our sleep in the vale
where we see each other home.

Better Not to Be Human

The accident of being human
leads to being mercenary
well-armed against the
moment and the sweat
with a frost-shielded lager
Held ice cold
for to be cool is key
in this open oven heat
of a fat-cheeked sun branding kisses
on the scarlet sealed
bottle in hand
tasting of safety
Czech
A roadside beleaguered by a deadpan horizon
of dead aphids bone flour torc scat

The alien tribute of the moon to sagebrush
through which quick-tempered gusts
roam and gang up with
desert
Present and place contrive a further on
that sinuous suggestion of solitude
its theme park and parades of
courage
Go on now so as not to give in
the prize of thought is heavy like perpetuity
even to the muscle-bound
soul

Past the mesa kingdom crowned with storm's
magenta thunder tide
red rock precisely mirrors westward
sunset's last notations inscribed
by the italicized junipers towards an
end

Tumbleweed wanders off the stage with the east
causing the habitual crime of
driving with headlights on
even when celestial doors swung open
fuse a star patch to rain
crashing down onto rivers of
sand

Into un-deified long-distance
trots the rib-cage coyote
on his lonely tangent under his
planetarium

In a wilderness of contradiction
he tests this cell of silence
runs, runs away from himself

Less animal than he wishes
over miles of dinosaur road he is
spellbound

A stream-lush canyon quivered and willowed
smiles back a sober welcome
unreliably, like a cat surmised in
last light

The vertigo of temptation spins
a yarn about growing roots
to stop the other spiral swallowed
by the amnesia of nothing

Ship Rock

The route driven straight and fast
bounces off parched platitudes
perceiving at each road sign
the hapless meander of life.
By the wayside, beached, a rock vessel
cuts shady tracks in the desert sand.
Crystal bleeds a lucent red
from mineral veins.
Ship, beast or gateway
near the long bare houses
satiated with heat
drying themselves clean in
the emaciated soil
stretching their thinly paneled hope
to this metaphysical shade
of obscure manufacture.
Crimson coolness. Utter desert.
Possessed by their hard blunt land
the bronzed people evaporate
into a death dream of rock
drawn up to a spirit-full sky
above shadow pools,
finding their bloodline anchor
and phantom archives amidst
ladder streams, ghost bells
rung, chorused, echoed
by flutings and archways.

Their oblong eyes burrowing
into the imaginative earth
beneath the surface desolation
that gnaws then rebuilds them.

Hall of mosses

The spiral of this sylvan spell
swivels both ways
to no beginning, no end,
on a loom of dizziness.
The maples capitalize their letters
on the immense page of my ignorance
harking back to the antediluvian era
of one primeval intuition.
I could sit here forever
at this tableland of slow motion,
sipping the broth of eons,
oddly at home,
though unsanctioned by these trees
ornate with annex germinations
combed with radiance, mist,
phosphorescence,
entranced beyond my reach,
unable to still their shadowy
perusal of millennia.

This inextricable realm
startles me into myopia and transience.
In a circle of their own
they resemble magi
with mandarin sleeves of moss.
Incandescent with implied wisdom
alien to man's eager climb
onto their thrones so as to rise
to their surfeit of time.

Swooning nearly
annihilated by a silence that
scrawls its might through me
initiated for an instant into a place
where terror and glory extend
a limb towards each other.

Above the Plain of Finnmark

Across the bleak polar sky
above the sullen icy sea
passes a solitary swan.
His lonely tempo resonates within me.
The contemptuous coast beyond
dark and low
perceives not this great innocence
lifted from oblivion
by the improbable persistence
of white beating wings.
I have flown past him
called by space
wide and opulent around
my own mental take-off.
The limitation and impermanence
of a single life suddenly shattered,
neither finite nor unique,
borrowed, borrowing, dissolving
into another's thoughts,
gaining substance from that one
sitting at a desk laden
like an Arab donkey
with uncertain feeling,
a porcelain cup, an oriental pot,
both as distant and fragile as
their anemic kaolin.
Irrepressible vagabond,

I travel to unnamed places
contrived from the commerce
between wake and sleep.
I am the figure of all the shadows
of my absence, a supposition verified
through latticed glimpses of the mind,
furtively uncovered by another consciousness
equally guessing at why she is there
in a possible place and time.
It is because the swan flies on
above the plain of Finnmark
bearing the dream of all dreams that is mine.

Art Full

High modernity
throws lateral glances
through the glass walls

of an airship apartment in which
a picture splashed on brightly,
is framed in licorice black
like a nocturnal New Yorker.

A fig sky hangs outside as tapestry
bruised by seasonal change.

Altitude and art gorge on metaphysics
in an anaconda room stretched out,
dappled marsh green and abysmal blue
under the lowered gaze of wood blinds.

Continents left their calling cards here
in a redolence of luxury.

Crimson insinuations escape the canvas
with candy stickiness.

A paint brush colors space and time
with indecisive March.

At every step guests forage through
a bric-a-brac of abstraction,

progress through an abundance
of deviations and parallelisms.

Who or what has been framed?
A fashion designer's trademark red,
a mechanic's oily wrench
a fallen empire of appliances
left on a futuristic wayside?

Through the window
in a last blast of brightness,

sunset, soon snuffed out
by minor chords from an insomniac piano.

Decoding

You exist, flattened by celluloid

and I am absent, simply non-existent.

Not a monochrome detail of that frozen scene
where other knights at the round table
turn away their heads,
gives me away to the future.

Now that I am alive
and you no longer so,
it seems a trompe l'oeil,
a ludicrous quid pro quo,
as if we'd never met.

Was it my insistent youth that chased you away?

Father, are you left on a bank of reeds where winter mourns?

Now I sit on that
same mildewed stool
dictating military code,
my back to naval maps,
the odd relay revealed
in our duplicate hands
gripping the microphone,
the same eagle hovering
over the ridge of our brow.

In war there is that
existential co-habitation
between the cold lull of fate
and the acute claim to life.

Do not die for an instant.
Set yourself free of the dated image,
nor disappear from any moment,
out-live all years that come and go.

Defiance against time
makes me stare.
You remain out of reach
with tight-lipped heroism,
a navy restraint locked onto you
not so much out of duty ,I know,
but from private disappointment.
No need to know why you volunteered
to join the carnage.
But I do because the veins
in our hands follow twin paths.

Let me dream in your place
by the grace of an innocence
that lingers in the tilt of your head,

let the Pacific rock your hammock
and its horizons decorate your eyes
through the palms where the south sea
rolls scaled like parrot fish.

Under the Leyte house you described,
bats fly out in dark droves
into the sunset's bishop garb,
to wreath your wishful night.

Out of that small island jungle
a barefoot child approaches you
and seeing you asleep,
invents your dreams.

Tropic

Heat soaks the mind:
an elliptical ocean of sweat
atop the skull of a gibbon.
Beyond cerebration and concern,
in geometric shadows,
white veils levitate and ventilate,
lava hair smoldering with rubies.
Drip drop, hush, the frost beads
on a sterling tumbler play ball
with a vermilion spider
as florid as a drunkard.
Menstruating earth leaks
liquors of corruption
into giant rivers
that usher mud and fleshy creepers,
sway raffiah tubs tethered to perspiring banks.
The crossed blades of lovers
screech in torment.
Hope's golden snake
lies lethal in a gutter,
and black-eyed despair,
pretty like a scarab,
grabs on to submission.

Camiguin

There you are at fear's end,
Mindanao's shadow darkening behind.
Island volcano smoking your thin idyll
with the sky like a solitary hero
puffing on the Gurkha Black Dragon
of a private triumph, calm, distant,
not one to get too close,
always contriving imminent departures
onto that tinseled streak of light
a fairy hand drew across the horizon.

Island that writes a far M
with the sea eagle's ballad wings,
the outlined mist and charcoal
of a simmering romance
where close-up, the jungle broods in green,
dolphins and swallows braid
their nose-dives of ordained beauty.
Woman stares at you burning
out her soul on your mirage,
that thirteenth dream of luck
far from the hoarse peddling of cities.
Waves roll at her feet like great cats
as she drifts into her self-cruelty:
far away island too, posing for another.
In the red scarred sky mauled by sunset
clouds pile on rumpled layers of drama
drawing a lone plume of smoke towards eruption.

Flash Frame

Last night I imagined a room
where I have been endlessly. In
a modernistic villa with colonial quips
on the edge of the South China Sea
hinged and knobbed with bronze
blinking white through latticed shutters
at afternoon's honeyed offing
across a bay's psychedelic dyes.

The sea side wall dismissed
by adventurous design construed
a lustrous fresco painting
a circus of island droplets
that cling to crescent beaches
propelling swimmers through cerulean swells.

Inside these high insular trusses
orchid clusters brand pinks
on coiled ropes in a glazed jungle
where skids the speckled monitor.

A parchment sunshine zooms in
on the steel knuckles of lean armchairs
melts tables smooth like ice floes
laps at creamy rug shores
on which bare feet go native.

A Mandarin blew gold powder
into the lacquered shade.
Surrealism glided in on a trade wind
dropping off Cocteau to draw
infinity in one unbroken line.

Of love the essence dresses me
in a constant summer.
In my pocket the red ink note
of a lion-eyed man with
a cat's observant poise.

A tropical hint of levity and tuberose
resets the heart.
In a dusk of paper lantern
and enameled sand
I savor a glint of moon
in night's cool drink.

The Archeologist gone mad

We are people of felt and fur
on which fibulae and breastplates
of bronze and gold reflect
the nomadic course of the sky.
Across our chests the sheep's horn
well used as cup or call.
Without such references who would I be?

For among these broad keen faces
I cannot distinguish my parents' features.

Around the fire we poke at freedom.
Nearby poplars shower yellow leaves
over the steely sinews of a river.
Beyond are reeds, honking lakes,
the fictile muscle of the tiger,
deserts where all conquerors have been
out-numbered by the proliferous stars.
The southeast mountains
poised like gods,
raise Olympian fortifications
to which we oppose our plains
without corners or alternatives.

Running, loving, dying
in one momentous rush,
led by light and the last dream,
careless of time's violence,

by day along the scent and rattle
of shallow streams, pursued
by wind that plaits the grass.

At night, from the disembodied remains
of those I can no longer see,
comes a silence that eludes distance
weaving nostalgia into speculation.
Am I Sabina, Larissa, Bermet?
I roll up the scroll of memory
to conclude my confusion.
I am Oulkhout,
rider of a pomegranate horse
in whose shadow trots
the giant sheep dog of the Turk
who shares my camel stew and sour milk.

I race with my own blood stream,
a million mysteries blown in my face.
I unlock a thousand locks of fortune.
Chronicler of the wayfarer and
accountant of countless planets
who in the darkness between them
asks the compulsory question:
who are you?

El Alto

I come into it as if condemned.
Sprung unborn,
undead, unhinged,
unplanned, in rubble
in constancy of chaos. Once
the fair soil of the Altiplano
now flagged with dust and nails.

Un-pedigreed monster
never put out of misery.
City that does not say
what it stands for.
Highland solitude robbed,
subjected to fits of madness.
Gone from these heights
the mystical view of a shaman's eye.

Excrescence deserted by animal spirits
and altitude's shyness,
hollowed by the neutered gaze
of the long-distance trucker.

In this storm of smog
lit by neon's canned glare,
some find a majesty,
a desolate drama of perdition.

But the disheveled and orphaned alleys
wave back with the loose tarps
over their grimacing windows.
Flap, flap, mantra of irrelevance.
In every street great agony before death.

The Far of Nowhere

In the far of nowhere the sky blown aloof
brings me to the edge of my body.

Outer forces indifferent to individuality
integrate my footprints.

Strident peaks initiate alien decibels,
with their scalpels cut out my substance,

freeing a renegade immensity
that has nor head nor tail.

Religions have decimated in armies
defeated by all this growth and decay.

The forest of nowhere safe
has long been travailed by glacier,

rippled and hummed by streams and a lake
cleft by upheaval and
tinged by wind's excrement.

The Saturnalian forest
fevered with creation,
is unbearably like human condition.

Carcass logs skinned bone white,
memorabilia left on the carnivorous beach
licking and devouring fiber with falsetto wavelets.

Collapsed trees efface themselves into soil
or with airs of shame, display monstrous tumors
and the same weary acceptance of anomaly.

A multitude of atoms pick at each other
in the on-going invention of beauty
insatiable for the warfare and tactics of love.

Giant

What does this mountain do all night
that I should know?
When a lunar snail slimes the glaciers
with a magnetic track of bullion,
a slow lick of hallucination?
When moon and earth lay close
together, composing appalling rhymes of
silence, the noiseless hammer of solitude
beating on the cold, still air?
What does this colossus do at night,
that makes me want to climb,
yet keeps me from leaving
the overturned image on the lake,
cosmic strand where intuitions
carve their names in ripples
and one of those may be mine?
A giant marauds through meadows
scented with milk-swollen cows
corralled by a rapt forest.
A huge chimera of kindness
haunts the dark woods.
Like all beautiful things
it shies away,
averse to capture.
The village slumbers
on banks neatly folded
by sleeping swans,
trusting in the titan.

Hints of Crime

The grimy smile of an archway
bridges houses of murder
in rows like lectured children or
prisoners being shot by a squadron.

Licked by the red tongue of a lantern
the street crooked with time has been
battered and crenelled by wheels
and winter's hard-bitten track.

Faceless windows stressed in brick
can no longer look straight
at the flower beds where
Spring gently comes of age.

Angels of nostalgia feathered the cobbles
in rapturous plummets.
Lyrical desolation ravished
the coziness behind the walls.

Snatched from a slice of iron sky,
a rush of stannic rain
saddens the pavement,
shadows the curb with shame.

Longing has no place to rest
but wanders in switchblade agony.
The passerby is filled with hollows,
suffering new wounds.

Gold and Other Treasure

A voice of forest comes to me from wells of silence:

the lure of a dripping fountain,
the caped brotherhood of contemplation.

A gilded utterance of autumn bursts from its treasure box
spraying gold leaves on a pillowed sky,

Aztec jeweled, cyanide blue
exhaled by mushroom and apple seed.

Highlights on the shadow palimpsest are
the first and last thought of oneself.

A naked marbled belief moves slowly
and every wood beast resounds as spirit in tune.

Near a Federal house leaves fall in a dark sonata

whose composer some time ago bowed
his head to the hastening of life.

Black pools lucid in their moss
mirror a solitude that rejoices in another

where dryads mutter deathless charms.

Metempsychosis

White mountaineering temple
looking up and away,
escalating a far-off idea.
A room's open windows reveal
a stage giddy with silence
and sun playing puppets
on dappled walls.
Even the feline skins
In their gilded frescoes
depart from the walls
out of lightness of heart,
rising above the melee.
In radiant dew, in claret robes,
monks of all ages scatter
over a lofty esplanade
losing all sense of place and time
to long weightless instants.
A silk-haired bodhisattva
in his dry blood wear,
alone on a scaffolding,
turns cat-faced
the kilns of his golden eyes
narrowed by mirth, and
as introduction, laughs with me.

Warped

Vapor on cloud streets,
I try to recall norms and rules
of substantiality. The sun
-dislocating a world of memories-
almost vanishes behind
a gray screen of incognito
in a pretense of final dissolution.
Through fog's mildew tarnished coins of
light here and there deny a total wipe-out.

A rocking horse, black maculae
painted on his bay flanks,
has trapped his head in the iron fence
of a pedestrian roundabout,
waiting for a child. Once free
he wars to be a Comanche horse.
In Arcanum's nearby alley, his stable
poorly covered in straw
like thinly buttered bread,
holds other members of his tribe
who, wound up by the time of day,
dilate pearly nostrils
to my conjuring hand.

I err from allegiance
to abjuration of absurdity
into a man's shop. Above the

counter the chiseled face
of a gothic angel or
a pantomime, entranced
by his own clutter.
Bronze buddhas, crystal cases,
moonstone beads, Netsuke,
rubies *en vrac*, bone marquetry coffers,
blue dragon carpets, red shawl
scrolled with gold thread rundles…
'Look!'his face says
'This all is me'. And when I leave
the pale claws of his longer arm
hold me back, his small
eclectic body a rare patchwork.
'Please talk to me a while'
he cries from deep within
this trance where beauty and horror
will not be set apart.

Meeting Again in the Tea Plantation

The invasive fog seeps
into her veins, down
the padded tea slopes,
coaxed by steep obsession
trailing a train of yonder,
dragging his image away
from her into death's murk,
feasting on her heart,
with cold command reaping
this crepuscule of the girl's
overtime hours. Lovelorn,
she does her work, clips,
harvests young leaves,
removes tenacious memories,
her gaze drained of color
in green acres of plantation.
Suddenly a rip in the brume
uncovers not six feet away
a face rogue yet innocent.
Despair allows her to see
through the golden whiskered mask.
The cursive spine spells
the first letter of his name.
It cannot be denied.
The resolute opal stare
helps her over
the line of species into
the wordless ecstasy
of their reunion.

At a Turn

Three thousand feet up
Still torn between skyward
And the chasmal green plunge
To the entomological swarm
Of the heat-pounded plain.
Dizzy with mounting steepness
Become the cosmic way
I gasp in syllables of mist
Password to the pylons ahead.
The high views through the giant I
Of the Dhupee tree
Sheds circumstantial laws.
Towards the peaks' gilded gaze
Tea plantations run and roll.
At a hairpin twist
Afternoon light burns through
All disbelief.
Suddenly you call me
Pervasive
On the roadside brimming
With petals and fern
In the medallion
Of a cottage window
Hung in a forest clearing.
A chink in the pavement
Has deviated me
Toward other truths.

Emotion beats at my temples
Nature is full of your fingertips.
Invisibly you shape the undeniable
From the improbable.
At a turn there can be no doubt.

ANOTHER VIEW

Just Before Dawn

White-winged window
flutters open
to the chill gasp
of adventure
of a night embalmed
in its blackest frame.
The city on its own
distills a vintage silence,
a wealth of emptiness
to walk the distance to its heart.

Nothing else matters now,
no other love compares.
Time and time again
in commas,
reels off shares of eternity
against the prudence of history.

You rejoin the classified intelligence
between stone, mortar
and the gorging
sea serpent tide.
Leaning against your own moonless pillar
pockets full of symbolisms
and the
intuition

that palaces and bridges
dizzy with elegance,
are spinning slowly off
into space
without chagrin.
The sympathy of the dead
no longer buried, radiates
from vaporous
upper floors.

Singularity wraps an intangible grace around you
in a habit of melancholy
lined with
euphoria.

You feel snug
next to the gentle horror
seeping through skinned masonry
in a dangled beauty
of hematic lanterns
and livid fog,
until dawn rubicund and fat with noise
severs the bond.

The Eel in the Mud

I.

The sun masked by a ballroom's moody splendor.

The glistening eel in the mud twists outside in.

I surrender to the old gold hours inside Venice.

Of its face nothing seen but the hollow eyes of windows

staring monsters into my corner of damask and brocade

where chocolate in a cup thickens to molten lava.

I sink into winter's inward tale found in halls

endless with marble, painted ceilings, ringing ducats,

the translucent schools of puffed chandeliers.

A forest rooted in viscosity grows a forlorn opulence

within me, misshaping the mind through its slimed griddle,

music exhaled by an introspective moon

in a semblance of death.

II.

Dawn's spreading galaxy. The silver gilt eel unwinds

into a seagull sky claiming a fresh hoard

of colors come in on the tide.

Daylight shoots iconoclastic prisms into the canals.

Churches cozy to angels and saints

holding on to their celestial riggings.

Solar intuition outlines crystal architectures.

Yesterday's curse recounted as a joke.

Ca'Dario sweats off its fever in a chalcedonic dew.

Spirits escape in flocks spinning towers into view,

streaking enchanted pathways for those who pray

and for those who never do.

Hakone Meditation

Around us the bedtime tale of a village
roof thatched and combed
by sprig fencing,
the parting of a path sprinkled
for punctilious cotton feet
turning the ruff heads
of Bonzai peonies
in the sharpened dusk
of black and white celluloid,
etched with nostalgia
for a recapitulated past
declaring polite defeat
while the frothing wave
of a returning tide unfurls,
wistful banner
on the night's samite breath.
We sit bare-minded
in deadly black
by a brook faking a cascade
under the eyeball of the moon
projecting a mess of trees
clawed and toothed
to guard contemplation.
We slip into absence and
mutual irrelevance,
confusing ourselves
with a perpetuity

by beauty bound:
frogs to the rustling stream,
crows hatched by shadow,
leaves breaking spring's shield,
shiver on a glimpse of insight.
A small crystal space
incubating between the lungs
has begun to dissolve
the last shreds of piety.
A scintillation blurs boundaries.
A stone's throw from an epicenter
as close as fear
of blanking out. But then
we resorb into pebbles,
throwing ourselves back
with hard twin plops
into water's footnote.

Dreaming of Joseph Conrad

Through sleep's dark ways a prelude to Joseph Conrad comes to
me
in jungle pageantry an island seed growing a flaring dawn.
My slumber wounded by an astral kriss healed by palmate
leafage
green with deluge.

The ache of foiled journeys departs at last on the tide of a tear
at the corner of my eye. Highbrow beardless his face clean cut
purified by adventure's call keen for solitary battles against black
storms
memory's rogue archaeology what people do to each other the
likes of which
are clearly exposed in the blue iris of the deep.

An emotion we share leans over the gunwale of a schooner
a constellation of nostalgia from a tie dye infancy of free
associations
gasps for open sea even as it stares down a fevered coast of
mangrove
dense with human psyche.

A mist of destinies in jonquil linen naval attire blossoms and wilts
waltzes briefly with luck ill-steps into madness. A scent of pipe smoke
wafts us over a sunny cove. Unaccountable time passes leveling all fates to a finish.

In the slatted shade of the tropics his hand in mine writes 'end'
yet the story just never ends.

Dreaming of Yukio Mishima

A half-naked man on a ledge
back to a warped pine

once a red cardinal bathing in snow
simulated a splash of blood

hears a recital of waves far below
plays the keyboard of his muscles
to a bleeding sunset

once the sshssh of silk across a floor
suggested an altered lust

an instant's acme barely inhabited
a rare brocade never worn

a room emptied by the western ticking of a clock
on the tangent of a drama
savored by the ritual mouth of an actor

each day stands on the cliff of age
stories stalk him like tigers

gold shapes into a vision of heaven
around which envy leaves bloody tracks

the unbearable ease of elegance breeds jealousy
in the cannibal heart of imitation

calm masculine with a Hollywood grace
weaving cigarette smoke into discipline

the house is the sharp blade of a sword
in formal uniform books in cosmic order

a smell of seaweed wafts from a coming storm
and youth is rescued by the salt taste of death

Within the Eye

He sketches, dabs, retouches,
in the painter's way.
At times in determined strokes,
scraping up dust, gas, star embryo, wind
he paints fluted greens for hydrogen,
ruby jet streams for sulphur,
blue eidolons for oxygen.
The black rim of his avid pupil
dilates and contracts to the light
of image where the pull
of the vacuum, just before
annihilation, is strongest.

For he always conceives,
tempted by destruction.
Partial to hyperbole,
subject to elation and depression
he brushes in three billion years
worth of shoulder and titanic muscle
loosely draped in atomic godliness.
What to make of this anarchy,
all these compressed and cleaving options?
A nearing fleet of wings creates immediate distance,
begins to flail light and darkness
that struggle to destroy each other.

In the stare spellbound by the canvas
of infinite space, gestates
the shape of authority
which extends an arm, finger
pointed at him. Obediently,
he commands a whole vault
to transmute into heaven.

Space Travel

No other way than a dreamer's
to exact a whim
from the open vowel of the sky
to deny time
in a last timely act
when the hour is right.

You cut the tube
lock yourself out
of how others remember you.
Your renegade thinking siphoned
into the black tulip of space
where your craft in aeronautic whites
dwindles to an asylum
for three-D delusions.

Seized by the animal powers of mystery
once held in the tiger's quasar eye
your solitude disperses like pearls
from a Duke's doublet
In a final adieu.
The old points of view
inhumed in a shell
of aluminum and polymers.

The 'us' of hush ushers you past
planets spinning kaleidoscopes of persona
through the held in breath of stillness.
Shaft after shaft of silence
cracks and roars so vastly
no echo can return.

Beyond Sedna's frozen stare
brains of heat seed singularities
armed with metals and fogs.
Shudder of twilight faintly lit
by gasping pulsars.

A nebular spiral
wedges in a recalled vertigo.

Blackness
fuses hammer and anvil.
The fathomless blank of subtraction
swallows you up.

The result of nothing spits you out,
twists you inside out
in a game from staggered rows of chance.
Abstraction ignites your infinite
in a constant waft of mutation.

A Poet's Birthday

October twenty-fourth 2075
It has been slow in coming,
taken this long to know better:
to be the accurate needle skimming
on mirrored currents of acuteness,
echo bouncing off light,
dormant energy immersed
in two verses at least,
high dive into liquid weaves
of color, scent, and consent
shot through by stupefaction undone,
no fit of lunacy could foretell.
No road signs, no fencing
in this endless hacienda of proverbial grass
sparkled with astral crickets,
magnetic with leas of hooves.
No destination, no departure,
no obstacles, no parting,
returns that compromise leaving.
No hapless exploration,
no added mileage granting you
privilege's widening smile.
Head pillowed by a phrenic breeze,
wonderment under a shower of clarity.

No weight, pulse or pressure,
no subjection, no reproduction,
all entangled disentangled where
speed and contemplation
stare each other down.
Directions taken, always untaken.
To go elsewhere, yet to remain.

Endless affinity in a field of stars.

From promise alerts long ago
to dells of a sympathetic ether.
Feline air cajoles runs off.
Dizziness shivers fragrant like rum cake,
tastes ethylic like a raspberry summer,
and of infinite expenditures of good luck.

You are now in the locus of dreams,
in the golden glow of their logic.
Yours, the madness of space
on a keel of exactitude.

Of somewhere else already
the captivating sapience.

About the Author

Stephanie V Sears is a dual national: French and American, born in Manhattan, NY, to an American diplomat/political analyst from Massachusetts and French mother from Aquitaine, France, who was employed at the French Ministry of Foreign Affairs and later at the UN. After first going to school in the United States in Massachusetts and Washington DC, Stephanie's high school years took place in France where she earned her Baccalaureate with honors. Much of her life after that has been a back and forth between both countries for university studies, family and professional reasons. She continues to share her time equally between both countries. Brought up in a culturally un-prejudiced family atmosphere, with a somewhat romantic sense of the world, it is no wonder that after a Masters at the Sorbonne (Paris V) in socio-history, she went towards ethnology (specializing in Polynesian cultures – specifically: the Marquesas Islands in French Polynesia) with a PhD (Doctorate) from the Ecole des Hautes Etudes en Sciences Sociales, Paris. As a pre-doctoral student and as a post-doctor she worked in several museums: in the United States (Metropolitan Museum of Art) and in France (Musee de l'Homme, Paris, Musee de la Castre, Cannes, Musee d'Histoire Naturelle, Colmar but also for a think tank in Paris involved in the promotion of democracy, and on a Peruvian project for Cultural Survival, in Boston. Her first publications were scholarly in nature, related to her thesis. Those first publications encouraged her to expand her focus to environmental issues and to the overall changing relationship between human society and wildlife, with occasional departures into more socio-cultural subjects. As an equestrian, horse cultures in Syria, Kirghizstan, Turkmenistan were also subjects of interest. An on-going love of adventure, possibly inherited from a long line of accomplished seamen on both sides of her family, and a curiosity for other cultural perspectives than her own, have led her to live in Hong Kong where she sold advertising space in a children's magazine, the Marquesas Islands, Barcelona where she wrote for the Barcelona Metropolitan, a local, English language, cultural tourism magazine: She also lived in New York, Paris, Boston and Verona. She continues to travel extensively throughout the world where landscapes, people, occasional odd circumstances have been a constant source of poetic and story-telling inspiration. Until now and by far, Central and East Asia and the Pacific islands have exerted their particular spell on her. Poetry became an interest at the age of fourteen, as an escape from algebra classes. The first lines written were no doubt heavily influenced by Arthur Rimbaud and written in French. Other admired poets include Byron, Eugenio Montale, Paul Valery, Rilke, Borges, Octavio Paz, Holderlin. This is by no means an exhaustive list of the poets she admires and keeps discovering, alive and dead. Later, she wrote poetry, once paternal reading suggestions in the great English Classic's but also in North and South American and Russian literature had made her more fluent in her second language, Her poems have been published in some forty literary magazines and reviews, with a Pushcart short-list nomination in the Hudson View, and two short-list nominations in Erbacce contests.

www.ingramcontent.com/pod-product-compliance
Lightning Source LLC
Chambersburg PA
CBHW032228080426
42735CB00008B/761
* 9 7 8 1 9 5 2 5 7 0 9 0 2 *